CARYL CHURCHILL

Caryl Churchill has written for the stage, television and radio. Her stage plays include *Owners* (Royal Court Theatre Upstairs, 1972); *Objections to Sex and Violence* (Royal Court, 1975); *Light Shining in Buckinghamshire* (Joint Stock on tour, incl. Theatre Upstairs, 1976); *Vinegar Tom* (Monstrous Regiment on tour, incl. Half Moon and ICA, 1976); *Traps* (Theatre Upstairs, 1977), *Cloud Nine* (Joint Stock on tour, incl. Royal Court, London, 1979, then Theatre de Lys, New York, 1981); *Three More Sleepless Nights* (Soho Poly and Theatre Upstairs, 1980); *Top Girls* (Royal Court, London, then Public Theatre, New York, 1982); *Fen* (Joint Stock on tour, incl. Almeida and Royal Court, London, then Public Theatre, New York, 1983); *Softcops* (RSC at the Pit, 1984); A *Mouthful of Birds,* with David Lan (Joint Stock on tour, incl. Royal Court, 1986); *Serious Money* (Royal Court and Wyndham's, London, then Public Theatre, New York, 1987); *Icecream* (Royal Court, London, 1989); *Mad Forest* (Central School of Speech and Drama, then Royal Court, London, 1990); and *Lives of the Great Poisoners* (with Orlando Gough and Ian Spink, Second Stride on tour, incl. Riverside Studios, London, 1991).

by the same author

CARYL CHURCHILL

THE SKRIKER

NICK HERN BOOKS
London

A Nick Hern Book

The Skriker first published in Great Britain 1994
as a paperback original by Nick Hern Books Limited,
14 Larden Road, London W3 7ST

The Skriker copyright © 1994 by Caryl Churchill

Front cover image: Man Ray photograph from
L'Amour Fou, Photography and Surrealism,
Hayward Gallery Catalogue, 1986

Typeset by Country Setting,
Woodchurch, Kent TN26 3TB

Printed by Cox and Wyman Ltd,
Reading, Berks

A CIP catalogue record for this book
is available from the British Library

ISBN 1-85459-275-0

Caryl Churchill has asserted her right to be
identified as the author of this work

The Skriker was first performed in the Cottesloe auditorium of the Royal National Theatre, London, with the following cast. The first preview was held on 20 January 1994 and the press night on 27 January 1994.

THE SKRIKER	Kathryn Hunter
JOSIE	Sandy McDade
LILY	Jacqueline Defferary
PASSERBY	Desiree Cherrington
YALLERY BROWN	Don Campbell
BLACK DOG	Brian Lipson
KELPIE / FAIR FAIRY	Philippe Giraudeau
GREEN LADY / JENNIE GREENTEETH	Lucy Bethune
GIRL WITH TELESCOPE / LOST GIRL	Melanie Pappenheim
HAG / WOMAN WITH KELPIE	Mary King
BOGLE / RAWHEADANDBLOODYBONES / DARK FAIRY	Stephen Goff
BROWNIE / RADIANT BOY	Richard Katz
MAN WITH BUCKET / NELLIE LONGARMS	Stephen Ley
SPRIGGAN	Robbie Barnett
GRANDDAUGHTER / BLACK ANNIS	Diana Payne Myers
GREAT-GREAT-GRANDDAUGHTER / DEAD CHILD	Sarah Shanson

Director	Les Waters
Designer	Annie Smart
Music	Judith Weir
Movement	Ian Spink
Lighting	Christopher Toulmin

Characters

THE SKRIKER
JOSIE
LILY

JOSIE and LILY are in their late teens

JOHNNY SQUAREFOOT
THE KELPIE
MAN WITH CLOTH AND BUCKET
YALLERYBROWN
PASSERBY
GIRL WITH TELESCOPE
GREEN LADY
BOGLE
SPRIGGAN
WOMAN WITH KELPIE
BROWNIE
DEAD CHILD
FAIR FAIRY
DARK FAIRY
RAWHEADANDBLOODYBONES
BLACK DOG
NELLIE LONGARMS
JENNIE GREENTEETH
BLACK ANNIE
HAG
LOST GIRL
BUSINESSMEN
THRUMPINS
BLUE MEN
PICNIC FAMILY

GRANDDAUGHTER
GREAT-GREAT-GRANDDAUGHTER

This is the script as originally written, before the beginning of the rehearsal process. There may be divergences between this script and the play as staged at the Royal National Theatre.

A speech usually follows the one immediately before it, BUT:

1) When one character starts speaking before the other has finished, the point of interruption is marked / as in

JOSIE.   They will / if you ask.

LILY.   I don't think so.

2) A character sometimes continues speaking right through another's speech, e.g.:

LILY.   Get away, you're crazy. / (*To* SKRIKER.) It's all

JOSIE.   It's her.

SKRIKER.   Mum, make her go away.

LILY.   right. (*To* JOSIE.) I never want / to see you .

JOSIE.   It's her.

THE SKRIKER

Underworld.

JOHNNY SQUAREFOOT, *a giant riding on a piglike man, throwing stones. He goes off.*

The SKRIKER, *a shapeshifter and death portent, ancient and damaged.*

SKRIKER. Heard her boast beast a roast beef eater, daughter could spin span spick and spun the lowest form of wheat straw into gold, raw into roar, golden lion and lyonesse under the sea, dungeonesse under the castle for bad mad sad adders and takers away. Never marry a king size well beloved. Chop chip pan chap finger chirrup chirrup cheer up off with you're making no headway. Weeps seeps deeps her pretty puffy cream cake hole in the heart operation. Sees a little blackjack thingalingo with a long long tale awinding. May day, she cries, may pole axed me to help her. So I spin the sheaves shoves shivers into golden guild and geld and if she can't guessing game and safety match my name then I'll take her no mistake no mister no missed her no mist no miss no me no. Is it William Gwylliam Guillaume? Is it John Jack the ladder in your stocking is it Joke? Is it Alexander Sandro Andrew Drewsteignton? Mephistopheles Toffeenose Tiffany's Timpany Timothy Mossycoat? No 't ain't, says I, no tainted meat me after the show me what you've got. Then pointing her finger says Tom tit tot! Tomtom tiny tot blue tit tit! Out of her pinkle lippety loppety, out of her mouthtrap, out came my secreted garden flower of my youth and beauty and the beast is six six six o'clock in the morning becomes electric stormy petrel bomb. Shriek! shrink! shuck off to a shack, sick, soak, seek a sleep slope slap of the dark to shelter skelter away, a wail a whirl a world away.

Slit slat slut. That bitch a botch an itch in my shoulder blood. Bitch botch itch. Slat itch slit botch. Itch slut bitch slit.

Put my hand to the baby and scissors seizures seize you sizzle. Metal cross cross me out cross my heartburn sunburn sunbeam in my eyelash your back. Or garlic lickety split me in two with the stink bombastic. Or pin prick cockadoodle do you feel it? But if the baby has no name better nick a name, better Old Nick than no name, because then we can have the snap crackle poppet to bake and brew and broody more babies and leave them an impossible, a gobbling, a no.

I've been a hairy here he is changeling changing chainsaw massacre massive a sieve to carry water from the well well what's to be done? Brother brewed beer in an eggshell. I said I'm old old every so olden dazed but I never see saw marjory before three two one blast off!

Put me on a red hot shovel pushel bushel and a peck peck peck. Gave me red hot metal in a piping hot metal in a pie ping pong what a stink. Call the vicar to exorcise exercise regular sex a size larger six or seventh heaven and hellcat.

Chopped up the hag whole hog higgledy pig in the middle. Kelpie gallops them into the loch stock and barrel of fun fair enough and eats them, falls out of the water into love with a ladylike, his head in her lap lap lap, her hand in his hairy, there is sand in it there is and there is sand and shells shock. Bloody Bones hides in the dark dark dark we all go into the dark cupboard love all. See through the slit where he sits on piles of bloody boney was a warrior and chews whom he likes. Dollop gollop fullup.

But they're so fair fairy fair enough's as good as a feast day. Take them by the handle and dance in the fairy ring a ring ding sweet for a year and a day date data dated her and never finished the first reel first real dance in the fairy ring on your finger and bluebell would wouldn't it. Their friends drag 'em out dragon laying the country waste of time gentlemen. Listless and pale beyond the pale moonlight of heart sore her with spirits with spirit dancing the night away in a mangy no no no come back again.

Eating a plum in the enchanted orchard, cherry orchid, chanted orchestra was my undoing my doing my dying my undying love for you. Never eat a fruit or puck luck pluck a flower if you want to get back get your own back get back to your own back to the wall flower.

When did they do what they're told tolled a bell a knell, well ding dong pussy's in. Tell them one thing not to do, thing to rue won't they do it, boo hoo's afraid of the pig bag. Open bluebeard's one bloody chamber maid, eat the one forbidden fruit of the tree top down comes cradle and baby. Don't put your hand in the fountain pen and ink blot your copy catching fishes eyes and gluesniffer. So he puts his hand in and wail whale moby dictated the outcome into the garden maudlin. Everything gone with the window cleaner.

Don't get this ointment disappointment in your eyes I say to the mortal middlewife but of course she does and the splendoured thing palace picture palace winter policeman's ball suddenly blurred visionary missionary mishmash potato, and there was a mud hit mad hut and the mother a murder in rags tags and bob's your uncle and the baby a wrinkly crinkly crackerjack of all trading places, because of course it was all a glamour amour amorphous fuss about nothing. But she never lets on so she gets home safe and sound the trumpet. But one day I'm in the market with b and put it in

the oven helping myself and she sees me and says
how's your wife waif and stray how's the baby?
And I say what eye do you seize me with? This
eye high diddley, she says. So I point my finger a
thing at her and strike her blind alley cat o' nine
tails.

Serve her right as raining cats and dogshit.
Whatever you do don't open the do don't open the
door.

I got a sweet sucker sweet till it melts in your
mouth. Watched the bride a cock horse in her
white lace curtain up trip through the grieve grove
graveyard rosy and honeysuckle on her daddy's
armour, lurked and looked till the groom for one
moribund strode up the pathtime. Hold this candle
the scandal I said, and he stood till it gutterbed
and went out. Then. What? No wedding party
frock! no broad no breed! no family life jacket
potato, no friends in need you ask! A hungered
yours hundred years later. And a bit a bite a bitter
bread and he was crumbs crumbling to dust panic.

Better forget them, not always be talking stalking
walking working them over and understand still.
Yes better forgotten rotten leaves them alone. We
don't need the knock kneed knead the dough re
mi fa away so there la di da. Never think shrink so
small about them at all a tall dark stranger than
friction. Then stop cockadoodle if you cancan.

They used to leave cream in a sorcerer's
apprentice. Gave the brownie a pair of trousers to
wear have you gone? Now they hate us and hurt
hurtle faster and master. They poison me in my
rivers of blood poisoning makes my arm swelter.
Can't get them out of our head strong.

Then get in their head body and tailor maiden has
a perfect fit a frit a fright a frying tonight jar.

We'll be under the bedrock a bye and by. We'll
follow you on the dark road at nightingale

blowing. No but they're danger thin ice pick in your head long ago away. Blood run cold comfort me with apple pie. Roast cats alive alive oh dear what can the matterhorn piping down the valley wild horses wouldn't drag me.

Revengeance is gold mine, sweet. Fe fi fo fumbledown cottage pie crust my heart and hope to die. My mother she killed me and put me in pies for sale away and home and awayday. Peck out her eyes have it. I'll give you three wishy washy. An open grave must be fed up you go like dust in the sunlight of heart. Gobble gobble says the turkey turnkey key to my heart, gobbledegook de gook is after you. Ready or not here we come quick or dead of night night sleep tightarse.

LILY *is visiting* JOSIE *in mental hospital.* LILY *is pregnant. Also there is the* KELPIE, *part young man, part horse.*

JOSIE.   I've a pain in my shoulder. I never used to have that did I. It's one of the things they give me here.

LILY.   I don't remember.

Pause.

Shall / I rub it?

JOSIE.   The food's not healthy. They put two things the same colour like white fish and mash potato.

LILY.   I could bring something in.

JOSIE.   I'm here to be punished.

LILY.   No, you were ill.

JOSIE.   Yes and I'm better now so can I come home with you?

LILY.   I don't think they'd let you.

JOSIE.	They will / if you ask.
LILY.	I don't think so.
	Pause.
JOSIE.	They will if you say you'll be responsible but you don't want to / be, do you.
LILY.	They wouldn't anyway.
JOSIE.	I don't blame you.
	Pause.
	All right, I will. I'll ask when I see the nurse. I'd love to take you out of here, Josie. I'd love it if I had a place of my own to take you and look after you, I'd love it.
JOSIE.	Why?
LILY.	Wouldn't you?
JOSIE.	I wouldn't love it, no. I'd do it.
	Pause.
LILY.	Have you made any friends here?
JOSIE.	I don't think so.
LILY.	What are the nurses like?
JOSIE.	I haven't noticed.
LILY.	Do they do things to you? I won't ask if you don't want. Like electrocute you. Or put you in a padded / cell or –
JOSIE.	They give me pills.
LILY.	What sort? what you got?
JOSIE.	That what you come for?
LILY.	No but if you / got some –
JOSIE.	I haven't got them, they've / got them.
LILY.	Take more when they're not looking, bring a whole lot out, be a laugh.

JOSIE.	You've no idea.
LILY.	What? what have I no idea?
	Pause.
	Nurse.
JOSIE.	No.
LILY.	What? Nurse.
JOSIE.	No.
LILY.	Don't you want to?
	Pause.
	Was she being naughty?
JOSIE.	You can't be naughty, a ten day old baby, can you. You really don't know anything / about
LILY.	I just meant she might have annoyed you.
JOSIE.	it. What can a ten day old baby do that's naughty?
LILY.	Like crying or – I don't know.
JOSIE.	You wouldn't kill a baby because it annoyed you, would you.
LILY.	I don't know.
JOSIE.	Would *you*?
LILY.	I don't know. You tell me.
JOSIE.	Of course you wouldn't.
	Pause.
LILY.	Was it difficult?
	Pause.
JOSIE.	Licence to kill, seems to me.
LILY.	You're in here.
JOSIE.	They don't hang you.
LILY.	They don't hang anyone.
JOSIE.	It should have been me that died.

LILY.   No, why?

Pause.

It's nicer here than I expected. The garden.

JOSIE.   You're thinking of going home.

LILY.   Not right away, no, but –

JOSIE.   Don't.

LILY.   I'm not.

JOSIE.   Take me with you.

LILY.   Josie, listen. I'm going to run away. But I'll write and tell you where I am, all right? I'm going to London.

JOSIE.   I won't hurt your baby.

LILY.   Of course not, I don't think that.

JOSIE.   If you'd got any sense you would. But you'd be wrong.

Pause.

Are you going then?

LILY.   No.

Pause.

JOSIE.   Wait till I tell you something.

Pause.

I thought it was a patient because if you saw them you'd know what I mean, there's some of them I'm nothing compared. You'd think I was worse because I've done something but some of them think they're someone else and I do know . . . What was I saying?

LILY.   You thought someone was / a patient.

JOSIE.   Yes but she's hundreds of years old. And then I was impressed by the magic but now I think there's something wrong with her.

LILY.   When you say hundreds of years old, you mean
            like eighty?

JOSIE.   She looks about fifty but she's I don't know
            maybe five hundred a million, I don't know how
            old these things are.

LILY.   When you say magic?

JOSIE.   I thought maybe she could go home with you.

LILY.   Josie, you'll be coming out soon. It's better to
            wait till they say.

JOSIE.   She'd like me to wish the baby back but I won't
            because she'd make it horrible.

LILY.   How do you know she's not a patient who just
            thinks she's . . .

            Pause.

JOSIE.   Rub my shoulder.

            LILY *rubs* JOSIE'*s shoulder.*

LILY.   When I get to the front gate is it left or right to the
            bus?

            She goes on rubbing her shoulder. She stops.

            All right?

            JOSIE *doesn't reply.*

LILY.   Josie?

            LILY *goes.* WOMAN *about 50 approaches.
            Dowdy, cardigan, could be a patient. It is the*
            SKRIKER.

SKRIKER.   I heard that.

JOSIE.   What?

SKRIKER.   You don't like me.

JOSIE.   I'm thinking what you'd enjoy and you'd like her
            better than me. She's stronger, she's more fun.
            I'm ill and I think you're ill and I / don't think –

SKRIKER.   You don't want me.

JOSIE. She'll have a baby and you'll like that.

SKRIKER. Please, please keep me.

Pause.

I'll give you a wish.

JOSIE. I don't want a wish.

SKRIKER. I'll be nice.

JOSIE. It's cold all round you.

SKRIKER. I can get you out of here. Just say.

JOSIE. No. Where to? No.

SKRIKER. Josie.

JOSIE. All right, I'll have a wish.

SKRIKER. Yes? Wish.

JOSIE. I wish you'd have her instead of me.

Pause. SKRIKER *turns away.*

Wait. I don't mind you any more.

SKRIKER. No, I'm not after you.

JOSIE. You won't hurt her? What do you want from her?

SKRIKER *starts to go. A* MAN *comes in carrying a white cloth and a bucket of water.*

Oh but I'll miss you now.

SKRIKER *goes.*

The MAN *spreads the cloth on the floor and stands the bucket of water on it. He waits. He isn't satisfied. He picks up the cloth and bucket and walks about looking for a better spot.*

Meanwhile the KELPIE *goes.*

YALLERY BROWN *is playing music.*

The MAN *puts the cloth and bucket down in another place. A derelict woman is shouting in the street. It is the* SKRIKER.

> *A* PASSERBY *comes along the street, throws down a coin, and then starts to dance to the music.*

> LILY *comes along the street.*

SKRIKER. What's the wires coming out of your head for? Collecting his brain in a box, mind you don't lose it. You've got a dead pig on your back.

> *She falls down in front of* LILY. LILY *helps her up.*

Can you help a poor old lady, lost my bus pass, price of a cup of tea, you've got a kind face darling, give you the white heather another time.

> LILY *gives her money and starts to go away but* SKRIKER *holds her.*

> *The* MAN *puts the cloth and bucket down in a new place.*

Do I smell? It's my coat and my cunt. Give us a hug. Nobody gives us a hug. Give us a kiss. Won't you give us a hug and a kiss.

> LILY *suddenly hugs and kisses her.*

There's a love. Off you go, Lily.

> SKRIKER *goes.*

> *The* MAN *is satisfied with the position of cloth and bucket and goes off without them.*

LILY. How do you know my name? – What? what's happening? my teeth. I'm sick. Help me. What is it? It's money. Is it? Out of my mouth?

> *Pound coins come out of her mouth when she speaks. She stops talking and examines the money.*

> A YOUNG GIRL *is looking through a telescope.*

> LILY *speaks carefully, testing.*

When I speak, does money come out of my mouth? Yes.

Through the telescope THE GIRL *sees a* GREEN LADY *dancing with a* BOGLE.

The PASSERBY *goes on dancing.*

LILY *goes.*

A YOUNG MAN, *who is a* BROWNIE, *comes in and starts sweeping and cleaning.*

The GREEN LADY *and* BOGLE *disappear when the girl looks away from the telescope. The* GIRL *looks again but they don't reappear. The* GIRL *goes.*

The PASSERBY *never stops dancing.*

SKRIKER *tells* LILY's *story.*

SKRIKER.   So lily in the pink with a finnyanny border was talking good as gold speaking pound coins round coins pouring roaring more and more, singing thinging counting saying the alphabetter than nothing telling stories more stories boring sore throat saw no end to it fuckit buckets and buckets of bloodmoney is the root of evil eye nose the smell hell the taste waste of money got honey to swallow to please ease the sore throat so could keep on talking taking aching waking all night to reach retch wrench more and more and more on the floor on the bed of a hotel tell me another not another wish it would stop stop talking now and sleep at last fast asleep and woke to find she can eek peak speak can I speak without can I without and about now changing the cash dash flash in the panic of time. And now in the hotel bar none but the brave deserve a drink I think for lily the

LILY *at a bar talking to an American woman of about 40 who is slightly drunk. It is the* SKRIKER. *There is a TV.*

There is a SPRIGGAN, *grotesquely ugly and ten foot tall, who is invisible to* LILY, *having a drink.*

Later the KELPIE *arrives. Then a* WOMAN *who drinks with the* KELPIE.

The BROWNIE *goes on cleaning. Later he finishes work and goes down on his hands and knees to lap a saucer of milk, then goes.*

SKRIKER.   So how does this work?

LILY.   How?

SKRIKER.   How does it –

LILY.   You want to turn it off?

SKRIKER.   No, how does that picture get here. From wherever.

LILY.   How does it *work*?

SKRIKER.   Yes.

LILY.   Oh you know, I don't know, you know, it's – isn't it the same in America?

SKRIKER.   Take your time. In your own words.

LILY.   It has to be plugged in so it's got power, right, electricity, so it's on so you can turn it on when you press the button, so the light's on and that shows it's on, ok?

SKRIKER.   But what's / the electricity – ?

LILY.   It's got all these tubes / and anyway –

SKRIKER.   No how do you see / all over the world?

LILY.   And meanwhile, let's say this is something live we're seeing, there's a camera there pointing at the picture at the thing that is the picture, camera, you want me to explain – the light gets in and there's the film, tape, the tape, it picks up the light somehow and it gets the picture *on* it, don't ask me, and there you are if it was a tape like you hire a tape down the video shop / that's it, they

SKRIKER.   No, tell me.

LILY.   make a whole lot of copies.

SKRIKER.   It's happening *there* and it's / *here*.

LILY.   I'm telling you, hang about, how it gets sent, I
can't quite, through the air, if it's live, or even if
it's not of course, if it happened before and they
recorded – say it's live, it's coming – not the
whole picture in the air obviously, it's in bits like
waves like specks and you need an aerial / to

SKRIKER.   This is crap.

LILY.   catch it and this changes it back into the picture /
and it's not a solid thing, it's all dots

SKRIKER.   But how for fuck's sake?

LILY.   and lines if you look, I can't help it. If it's on the
other side of the world they bounce it off a
satellite yes I'm explaining satellite which is a
thing a thing they put up in space ok, they put it
up I'm explaining that too and it's going round
like a star, stars don't go round, like a moon but it
looks like a star but moving about you sometimes
see it at night, and it bounces off the satellite / all
right –

SKRIKER.   What bounces off?

LILY.   The picture.

SKRIKER.   The picture bounces off?

LILY.   The waves, the – what is this?

SKRIKER.   You're holding out on me.

LILY.   I don't have all the technical if you want the
jargon if you want the detail you'll have to ask
someone else.

SKRIKER.   Don't fuck with me.

LILY.   Look, / that's all I –

SKRIKER.   And flying. I suppose / you don't know

LILY.   What?

SKRIKER.   how you fly? / And the massive explosions that –

LILY.   I don't fly.

SKRIKER.   No idea, huh? Never fly, never flown / across the
            sea –

LILY.   Fly you mean go in a plane no but even if I had / I
            wouldn't –

SKRIKER.   Or how you make poisons?

LILY.   What?

SKRIKER.   You people are killing me, do you know that? I
            am sick, I am a sick woman. Keep your secrets,
            I'll find out some other way, I don't need to know
            these things, there are plenty of other things to
            know. Just so long as you know I'm dying, I hope
            that satisfies you to know I'm in pain.

LILY.   Are you ill? Can I help? / Can I get something?

SKRIKER.   No no no, forget it. Really.

LILY.   You're in pain?

SKRIKER.   Not at all, no, I'm just fine, forget it. I don't have
            much aptitude for science. I guess you don't
            either. No big deal. We can just watch what
            comes over.

            Pause.

LILY.   You feel all right?

SKRIKER.   You are a sweet girl. You are just such a sweet
            girl.

            Pause.

            Running away from home is a great start. I did it
            myself. It can get to be a habit. You keeping the
            baby?

LILY.   Yes of course.

SKRIKER.   Because I'm looking for one, no I'm kidding.
            Look at it floating in the dark with its pretty
            empty head upside down, not knowing what's
            waiting for it. It's been so busy doubling doubling

and now it's just hovering nicely decorating itself with hair and toenails. But once it's born it starts again, double double, but this time the mind, think of the energy in that. Maybe I could be the godmother.

LILY.   You're staying in London?

SKRIKER.   Do you have friends in London?

LILY.   No but –

SKRIKER.   You now have one friend in London. And I have one friend in London. Ok? Not ok?

LILY.   Yes yes I do want to be friends. I just –

Pause.

SKRIKER.   Anyone would think you were frightened of me. I'm frightened of you.

LILY.   You're the one Josie said.

SKRIKER.   But I want to be friends.

LILY.   Why am I frightening?

SKRIKER.   Lily, I'll level with you, ok? You ready for this? I am an ancient fairy, I am hundreds of years old as you people would work it out, I have been around through all the stuff you would call history, that's cavaliers and roundheads, Henry the eighth, 1066 and before that, back when the Saxons feasted, the Danes invaded, the Celts hunted, you know about any of this stuff? Alfred and the cakes, Arthur and the table, long before that, long before England was an idea, a country of snow and wolves where trees sang and birds talked and people knew we mattered, I don't to be honest remember such a time but I like to think it was so, it should have been, I need to think it, don't contradict me please. That's what I am, one of many, not a major spirit but a spirit.

LILY.   And why are you here?

SKRIKER.   I am here to do good. I am good. You look as if you doubt that.

LILY.   No, of course not.

SKRIKER.   I am a good fairy.

LILY.   You do good magic?

SKRIKER.   That's exactly what I do.

LILY.   And you'll do it for me?

SKRIKER.   Where do you think your money comes from?

LILY.   I'm not ungrateful.

SKRIKER.   You're the one I've chosen out of everyone in the world.

LILY.   Why?

SKRIKER.   Because you're beautiful and good. Don't you think you are? Yes everyone sometimes thinks they're beautiful and good and deserve better than this and so they do. Are you telling me I made a mistake? I'd be sorry to think I'd made a mistake.

LILY.   No. No I'm glad.

SKRIKER.   And you accept?

LILY.   What?

SKRIKER.   Accept my offer. Accept my help.

LILY.   Yes. I think – what offer?

SKRIKER.   My help.

LILY.   Do I have to do something?

SKRIKER.   Just accept my help, sweetheart.

    Pause.

LILY.   No, I . . . It's very kind of you but . . . I don't like to say no but . . .

SKRIKER.   You might as well say yes. You can't get rid of me.

LILY.   No.

SKRIKER.   Who the fuck do you think you are?

Pause.

Whatever you say.

LILY.   You should have stayed with Josie. She's braver than me.

SKRIKER.   She wished I'd go with you.

LILY.   Did she? I wish she'd come and help me then.

SKRIKER.   That's the way. You'll begin to get a taste for it.

LILY.   For what?

SKRIKER.   Wishes.

LILY.   I didn't –

SKRIKER.   Yes.

Pause.

Tell me how the TV works and I'll trade.

LILY.   I don't know how the TV works.

SKRIKER.   Would you like a ring that when you look at the stone you can tell if your loved one is faithful?

LILY.   I don't have a loved one.

SKRIKER.   I can fix that, no problem. Just tell me how / the TV –

LILY.   I don't know how the TV works.

LILY goes.

The WOMAN gets on the KELPIE's back and rides off.

SPRIGGAN goes. SKRIKER goes.

The MAN comes back to his bucket and cloth. He skims a gold film off the top of the water in the bucket which he makes into a cake. He puts the cake on the cloth, draws a circle around it and sits down to wait. The PASSERBY is still dancing.

A DEAD CHILD *sings.*

DEAD CHILD.

My mother she killed me and put me in pies
My father he ate me and said I was nice
My brothers and sisters they picked my bones
And they buried me under the marley stones.

Derelict WOMAN *muttering and shouting in the street. It is the* SKRIKER. JOSIE *comes by.*

SKRIKER.   I know my son is writing me letters all the time and the army is stopping them because the officers are devils and do what you tell them because they are DEVILS and the letters are in sacks in the Bank of England waiting for the Day of Judgment when you will go to HELL and lose sight of me and stop moving me about but you can't move me now because my fingers are just so because I'm in charge of the devils and if I keep it up the devils will let my son go LET MY SON GO. What are you staring at?

JOSIE.   You.

SKRIKER.   Can you spare the price of a cup of / tea darling

JOSIE.   No.

SKRIKER.   because I haven't eaten all day, bless you for a sweet kind face. / I haven't eaten today but never

JOSIE.   I said no.

SKRIKER.   mind if you've no money my darling, that happens to all of us, just give me a kiss instead. Won't you give me / a kiss sweetheart?

JOSIE.   Get off, you stinking crazy –

SKRIKER.   You're a nasty girl, Josie, always were.

SKRIKER *goes*

JOSIE.   Is it you, come back, you – What? uh uh I'm sick, what, it's alive, it's – it's toads is it, where from, me is it, what?

As she speaks toads come out of her mouth. She speaks carefully, testing.

When I speak, do toads – ?

They do.

She opens her mouth to cry out in rage after SKRIKER, and shuts it, forcing herself to be silent to prevent more toads. She goes.

A FAIR FAIRY comes and tries to pick up the cake, the MAN won't let her have it, she goes. He sits waiting. The PASSERBY is still dancing.

JOSIE and LILY are sitting on a sofa. LILY is wrapped in a blanket. The SKRIKER is part of the sofa, invisible to them.

During this, a DARK FAIRY tries unsuccessfully to get the cake.

JOSIE.   So you think it was just her got me out?

LILY.   Because I wished it.

JOSIE.   No I'm better, that's why.

LILY.   And they bought you a train ticket?

JOSIE.   They do that when they discharge you from hospital.

LILY.   And how did you bump into me in the street?

JOSIE.   Because I'm lucky.

Pause.

JOSIE.   Aren't you glad to see me?

LILY.   I don't feel very well. Is it cold in here?

JOSIE.   No, it's fine.

LILY.   I'm freezing.

JOSIE.   You must be ill then.

LILY.   Yes, I think I am.

JOSIE.   Or that could be her.

Pause.

LILY.   What could?

JOSIE.   She's cold.

LILY.   I'm cold because I'm ill, all right?

JOSIE.   All right.

          Pause.

JOSIE.   Toads. She thinks she's funny. She's got it coming.

          Pause.

LILY.   Don't you think it's sad . . .

JOSIE.   What?

          Pause.

LILY.   I think I'm fainting.

          Pause. LILY *touches* SKRIKER.

          Josie, there's something icy.

JOSIE.   You better go to bed.

LILY.   There's a thing. It's got a face.

JOSIE.   Stop it.

LILY.   Feel.

JOSIE.   No.

LILY.   I can see her. Josie, see her, you must.

JOSIE.   She's for you now. You took her money.

LILY.   No, I can't bear it, I wish / you'd –

JOSIE.   Don't.

LILY.   I wish you'd see her too.

          Pause.

JOSIE.   So I see her, so what?

SKRIKER. Josie's not frightened.

JOSIE.   Toads, what you do that for, I'm not toads inside,
          it's you that's toads.

SKRIKER leaps up out of the sofa. She's wearing a short pink dress and gauzy wings.

SKRIKER.   Here I am as you can see
A fairy from a Christmas tree.
I can give you heart's desire
Help you set the world on fire.

LILY.   This is a dream, it's a nightmare and I'll wake up. I know I think other things happened like the money but that's because I'm remembering it in the dream.

JOSIE.   It's not a dream. She made me / speak toads.

LILY.   You would say that because you're just somebody in my dream.

JOSIE.   I'm not, it's me, I'm awake.

SKRIKER.   Don't you want a wish, Lily?

LILY.   I'll tell you about it in the morning.

SKRIKER.   What would you like, Lily?

JOSIE.   Lily, / be careful.

LILY.   I can't wake up yet but I can make it stop being a nightmare.

JOSIE.   Lily –

LILY.   I wish for flowers.

Flowers fall from above. SKRIKER takes LILY's hand and puts it against her face.

SKRIKER.   I'm warmer now, feel.

LILY.   And if it's not a dream it's even better.

The GREEN LADY comes for the cake. The MAN gives it to her and she eats it. They go off together. The PASSERBY goes on dancing.

There is a row of small houses. The SPRIGGAN and RAWHEADANDBLOODYBONES tower over them.

A BLACK DOG.

LILY *is in a park. A* SMALL CHILD *approaches her. It is the* SKRIKER.

THE GIRL WITH THE TELESCOPE *is looking through it but not seeing the* GREEN LADY. *She is tired and sad.*

LILY.　　Can you play cat's cradle?

SKRIKER *shakes her head.*

Shall I show you?

SKRIKER *nods.* LILY *shows her cat's cradle.*

Put your fingers in here and take it. Good. Now I take it back. Now put your fingers, see, in there. Careful, that's it. Now I take it. Now you – that's right. This one's called fish in a dish. You use your little fingers and cross over – Oh it's all in a tangle.

SKRIKER.　Do it again.

LILY.　　I'll show you one you can do by yourself.

LILY *does it,* SKRIKER *watches.* JOSIE *comes and watches too.*

LILY.　　There, do you like that?

SKRIKER.　Show me again.

LILY.　　Watch what I'm doing. Get it like this to start. What's your name?

SKRIKER.　I can do it. / Let me do it.

LILY.　　Wait. Where do you live?

SKRIKER.　In the flats.

LILY.　　Have you got any brothers and sisters?

SKRIKER.　Are you going to have a baby?

LILY.　　Yes.

SKRIKER.　When?

LILY.　　Soon. There, do you like that?

LILY *shows* SKRIKER *the cat's cradle.*

SKRIKER.   Can I be its sister?

LILY.   You can't really be its sister.

SKRIKER.   I can, I can be, please let me. I want a baby, I want a baby brother or a baby sister.

LILY.   You'll have to ask your mum to have a baby.

SKRIKER.   I haven't got a mum. Please let me be a sister. Say yes. Say yes. Please say yes.

LILY.   Yes all right.

SKRIKER.   I'll be its sister and you can be my mum.

LILY.   Who do you live with?

SKRIKER.   Please say yes. Pretend.

LILY.   I'll be your pretend mum.

SKRIKER.   Will you give me real dinner or pretend dinner?

LILY.   Pretend dinner.

SKRIKER.   Real sweets or pretend sweets?

LILY.   I might find / some real sweets.

JOSIE.   Do you like this child?

SKRIKER.   Where? / Get some now. What kind?

LILY.   Yes, I do.

JOSIE.   She's horrible. There's something wrong with her.

JOSIE *takes hold of* SKRIKER *to look at her.*

LILY.   Leave her alone.

SKRIKER.   Leave me alone, I'll tell my mum.

JOSIE.   She's not your mum. You haven't got a mum.

SKRIKER.   Mum! mum!

LILY.   Josie, stop it. It's all right, pet, she's just / teasing.

JOSIE.   Get out you little scrounger. / Leave Lily alone.

SKRIKER.   Mum, don't let her / hit me.

LILY.   Josie.

JOSIE.   I know you, you bastard. How you like toads? you like dirt in your mouth? Get away from us. You come in the house I'll put you in the fire, then we'll see what you look like.

JOSIE picks up dirt from the ground and stuffs it in the SKRIKER's *mouth.* LILY *rescues* SKRIKER.

LILY.   Get away, you're crazy. / (*To* SKRIKER.) It's all

JOSIE.   It's her.

SKRIKER.   Mum, make her go away.

LILY.   right. (*To* JOSIE.) I never want / to see you.

JOSIE.   It's her.

LILY.   Of course it's not her, it's a child, you're mad, you should have stayed in hospital, I can't look after you, you go round attacking people they'll take you away again and I won't care, I won't help you get out next time, / now go away and leave us alone.

JOSIE.   She can have you then, I don't care, I'm not helping you.

JOSIE goes further away and watches.

LILY.   Let's wipe your mouth. Poor baby. Did she hurt you? Nasty Josie.

SKRIKER.   Nasty Josie. Nasty Josie. Nasty Josie.

LILY.   Now where's our piece of string?

SKRIKER.   Give me a cuddle. Let me sit on your lap.

LILY.   Careful, mind my tummy.

SKRIKER.   You're fat.

LILY.   It's the baby.

SKRIKER.   I'm the baby.

LILY.   No, you're the baby's big sister.

SKRIKER.   Fat fat fat.

LILY.   Careful.

SKRIKER.   Nasty baby.

           She hits LILY'*s stomach.*

LILY.   Don't. Get off.

SKRIKER.   Mum. Mum.

LILY.   Come on then but be careful. Don't hurt the
           baby.

SKRIKER.   Cuddle.

LILY.   Cuddle cuddle.

SKRIKER.   Kiss.

           LILY *kisses her.*

LILY.   Better now?

SKRIKER.   Let's go home.

LILY.   Home where?

SKRIKER.   Where we live.

LILY.   This is our house here.

SKRIKER.   No I mean go home. To your house.

LILY.   I better not take you back there. Someone's going
           to wonder where you are.

SKRIKER.   No one's going to wonder. I want to go home.
           Take me home.

LILY.   Let go, you're / pulling my hair.

SKRIKER.   No no, hold me. Hold me.

LILY.   Get down, / let go. Mind the baby.

SKRIKER.   Hold me tight.

LILY.   Let go. I'm telling you. / Now let go.

SKRIKER.   Never never never / never.

LILY.   You'll get a smack. Now get off. You're hurting.
           Get off.

           She hits SKRIKER *and pushes her away.*
           SKRIKER *lies on ground crying.* JOSIE *comes*
           back.

           Have I hurt her?

JOSIE.   Not enough.

           SKRIKER *sits up.*

SKRIKER.   You touch me I'll tell my dad you'll be sorry, get
           my brother on you he's bigger than you, I got lots
           of friends / everywhere set them on you watch out
           get in your head get in your eyes turn you into
           dogshit on my shoe.

JOSIE.   What you hurt me for, toads, what you do that for,
           I was looking for you, I'm not frightened, you're
           frightened, only did toads when I wasn't ready
           I'm ready now you just try you're no good there's
           something wrong with you you're a spastic fairy
           you need us more than we need you should have
           thought of that / before you done that to me too
           late.

LILY.   Josie, it's not.

SKRIKER.   You're stupid, aren't you, Lily. Josie knows.

JOSIE.   Leave her alone, she can't – . You can come back
           to me.

SKRIKER.   I don't want to. I like Lily.

JOSIE.   But I wish it.

SKRIKER.   I don't have to do what you wish. Lily doesn't
           wish it, do you?

LILY.   I don't know.

SKRIKER.   No because I might give you nice things. And
           Josie wants nice things. That's why she wants
           me. Not to help Lily. So you both want me. /
           That's nice.

LILY.   I don't, no I don't.

SKRIKER.   Josie's not frightened.

JOSIE.   What do you want?

SKRIKER.   I want a lot but so do you. We could both have it.

JOSIE.   Have what?

SKRIKER.   Whatever you like.

LILY.   Josie, don't do it. When you feel her after you it's . . . Josie, remember what it felt like / before, don't do it.

JOSIE.   But when you've lost her you want her back. Because you see what she can do and you've lost your chance and it could be the only chance ever / in my life to –

LILY.   Josie, don't.

SKRIKER.   I knew you were desperate, that's how I found you. Are you ready now?

LILY.   Josie, I wish / you wouldn't.

SKRIKER.   You don't count any more.

           Pause.

JOSIE.   Yes.

           Blackout. A horrible shriek like a siren that goes up to a very high sound and holds it. Gradually it relents little by little breaking up into notes and coming down till it is pleasant and even melodious.

           Underworld. As SKRIKER *and* JOSIE *arrive it springs into existence. Light, music, long table with feast, lavishly dressed people and creatures, such as* YALLERY BROWN, NELLIE LONGARMS, JENNY GREENTEETH, THE KELPIE, BLACK DOG, RAWHEADAND-BLOODYBONES, THE RADIANT BOY, JIMMY SQUAREFOOT, BLACK ANNIS (with a blue face and one eye). It looks wonderful* *except that it is all glamour and here and there it's not working – some of the food is twigs, leaves, beetles, some of the clothes are rags, some of the beautiful people have a claw hand or hideous face. But the first impression is of a palace. SKRIKER is a fairy queen, dressed grandiosely, with lapses.*

As they arrive the rest burst into song. Everyone except JOSIE and the SKRIKER sings instead of speaking. They press food and drink on JOSIE, greet her, touch her.

SPIRITS.   Welcome homesick
drink drank drunk
avocado and prawn cockfight cockup cocksuck
red wine or white wash
champagne the pain is a sham pain the pain is a sham
fillet steak fill it up stakes in your heart
meringue utang
black coffee fi fo fum.

A HAG rushes in shrieking. She seizes food, scattering it, searching. She sings.

HAG.   Where's my head? where's my heart? where's my arm? where's my leg? is that my finger? that's my eye.

The SPIRITS laugh and jeer at her and repeat what she says, singing.

SPIRITS.   Headlong . . . heartthrob . . . harmful . . . legless . . . finicky . . . eyesore.

HAG.   Give me my bones.

JOSIE and SKRIKER speak, everyone else sings.

JOSIE.   What is it? what's the matter?

HAG.   They cut me up. They boiled me for dinner. Where's my head? is that my shoulder? that's my toe.

SKRIKER.   They chopped her to pieces, they chipped her to

pasties. She's a hag higgledepig hog. She's a my my miser myselfish and chips.

SPIRITS.   A miser a miserable

HAG.   Give me my bones.

The SPIRITS jeer and pelt the HAG with bits of food and drive her away.

They repeat previous singing about the feast. A lost girl takes JOSIE aside and sings to her under cover of the other singing.

GIRL.   Don't eat. It's glamour. It's twigs and beetles and a dead body. Don't eat or you'll never get back.

The SPIRITS urge food on JOSIE and the GIRL has to move away. But she manages to get back.

Don't drink. It's glamour. It's blood and dirty water. I was looking for my love and I got lost in an orchard. Never take an apple, never pick a flower. I took one bite and now I'm here forever. Everyone I love must be dead by now. Don't eat, don't drink, or you'll never get back.

SPIRITS push her aside and sing on, louder and more chaotically. SKRIKER offers JOSIE a glass of red wine.

SKRIKER.   Your wealth, Josie, happy and gory.

JOSIE.   I'm not thirsty.

SKRIKER.   Thirst and worst, mouth drouth dry as dustbowl.

JOSIE.   Yes, but I don't –

SKRIKER.   Dizzy dozy chilly shally.

JOSIE.   Yes but I don't want –

SKRIKER.   Don't you want to feel global warm and happy ever after? Warm the cackles of your heartless. Make you brave and rave. Look at the colourful, smell the tasty. Won't you drink a toasty with me, Josie, after all we've done for?

JOSIE *drinks. Everyone is silent and attentive for a moment. Then they all burst out singing again triumphantly, among them* THE GIRL *sings.*

GIRL. Twigs and beetles and dead body. Water and blood. You'll never get back.

But JOSIE *doesn't notice her. She is happy now and eats the food they pile in front of her, not noticing the difference between cake and twigs. The* SPIRITS *celebrate, congratulating the* SKRIKER.

SPIRITS. We won wonderful
full up at last
last man's dead.

One by one the spirits get up and dance, and JOSIE *and the* SKRIKER *too, increasing frenzy. Some of them fly into the air.*

In the confusion the feast disintegrates. Finally everything and everyone has gone except the PASSERBY *still dancing.*

Silence and gloom. JOSIE *appears on her hands and knees scrubbing the floor. A* MONSTER *comes to watch her. It is the* SKRIKER. *There is a fountain.*

SKRIKER. Better butter bit of better bitter but you're better off down here you arse over tit for tattle, arsy versy, verse or prose or amateur status the nation wide open wide world hurled hurtling hurting hurt very badly. Wars whores hips hip hoorays it to the ground glass. Drought rout out and about turn off. Sunburn sunbeam in your eye socket to him. All good many come to the aids party. When I go uppety, follow a fellow on a dark road dank ride and jump thrump out and eat him how does he taste? toxic waste paper basket case, salmonelephantiasis, blue blood bad blood blue blood blad blood blah blah blah. I remember dismember the sweet flesh in the panic, tearing

limb from lamb chop you up and suck the
tomorrow bones. Lovely lively lads and maiden
England, succulent suck your living daylights,
sweet blood like seawater everywhere, every bite
did you good enough as good as a feast.

JOSIE.   And now no one tastes any good?

SKRIKER.   Dry as dustpans, foul as shitpandemonium.
Poison in the food chain saw massacre.

JOSIE.   If I could just go and see. I'd come back.

SKRIKER.   Shall I take you in my pocket pick it up and tuck
it in?

JOSIE.   Yes please.

SKRIKER.   Up in the smokey hokey pokey? up in the world
wind? up in the war zone ozone zany grey?

JOSIE.   Because it's years. I think I've lived longer than
they do up there. If I don't go now I won't know
anyone.

SKRIKER.   What will you pay me say the bells the bells?

JOSIE.   Sip my blood?

SKRIKER.   Haven't I sipped lipped lapped your pretty twist
wrist for years and fears? What's happy new,
what's special brew hoo?

JOSIE.   I had a dream last night.

SKRIKER.   Haven't I wrapped myself up rapt rapture
ruptured myself in your dreams, scoffed your
chocolate screams, your Jung men and Freud
eggs, your flying and fleeing? It was golden olden
robes you could rip tide me up in but now it's a
tatty bitty scarf scoff scuffle round my nickneck.
Give a dog a bone.

JOSIE.   Tell you something I remember.

SKRIKER.   Haven't I drained rained sprained ankles and
uncles, aunts and answers, father and nearer?

What do you know about your selfish you haven't worn down out?

JOSIE.   Got a new one.

SKRIKER.   Bran tub new? lucky dipstick?

JOSIE.   Never even thought it myself. Something I saw when I was three.

SKRIKER.   What?

JOSIE.   Will you take me up?

SKRIKER.   What?

JOSIE.   A little bit of stony ground.

SKRIKER.   And?

JOSIE.   It had little stones on it.

SKRIKER.   Were you alonely?

JOSIE.   I don't remember. Probably alone. No, probably someone nearby. I remember the stones.

SKRIKER.   What can I do with a scrap crap wrap myself up in it? Ground to a halt. Stone death.

JOSIE.   But you'll take me with you?

SKRIKER.   That doesn't bye bye a trip up. You're dry as dead leaves you behind.

JOSIE.   Please.

SKRIKER.   You'll never go home on the range rover's return again witless.

JOSIE.   Why not, if I'm useless?

SKRIKER.   When I'm weak at the need, you'll be a last tiny totter of whisky whistle to keep my spirits to keep me stronger linger longer gaga. And while I'm await a minute, don't touch the water baby.

JOSIE.   Don't touch the water in the fountain because I'll die.

           SKRIKER *goes*.

JOSIE goes to the fountain and almost puts her hand in the water.

She shrieks and plunges her hands in. A shrieking sound gets louder and louder.

Darkness.

JOHNNY SQUAREFOOT *throwing stones at* BLACK DOG.

JOSIE, LILY *and the* SKRIKER *as child are exactly as they were in the park.* SKRIKER *runs off.*

The BLACK DOG *is in the park. The* GIRL WITH THE TELESCOPE *sits depressed. The* KELPIE *and the* WOMAN *who rode off on his back stroll as lovers.*

LILY   (*shouting after* SKRIKER). We're not scared of you.

                (*To* JOSIE.) It's just a child anyway.

JOSIE.   Too bright. No it's bright there. My eyes don't work. Hold me.

LILY.   Now what?

JOSIE.   You smell like people. Your hair's like hair. It was like putting a gun to my head because they always said I'd die if I did that. Liars, you hear me? I got away. Yah. Can't get me.

LILY.   Stop it. You can stop it.

JOSIE.   I was ready to die. I thought I'd never get back.

LILY.   Don't. It makes me lonely.

JOSIE.   That's right I'm not dead? We're not both dead? Lily, you didn't die while I was away?

LILY.   Josie.

JOSIE.   No, tell me are we dead?

LILY.   No we're not. Stop it.

JOSIE.   How long's it been?

LILY.   How long's what?

JOSIE.   I went for.

LILY.   Come on, let's go home.

JOSIE.   I had a whole life. How long? I'm very old.

LILY.   You went? what?

JOSIE.   Years and years, longer than I lived here, I wasn't
         much more than a child here hardly. I've got
         children there, Lily, and they're grown up but I
         didn't mean to leave them, I thought I'd just die,
         won't I ever see them? I don't want to go back.
         How can I live now?

LILY.   You can't be old. Look at you. Look at me.

JOSIE.   Yes, how do you do that? You've travelled into
         the future. You're not real. You're something
         she's made up.

LILY.   Josie. (LILY *hugs her*.)

JOSIE.   Are you glad to see me?

LILY.   I never stopped seeing you.

JOSIE.   But you're glad?

LILY.   Yes.

JOSIE.   When is this? I don't know when it is.

LILY.   It's just today like it's been all day. We went to
         the shops. We met a child in the park.

JOSIE.   That's horrible.

LILY.   Please, I'm tired. My stomach hurts.

JOSIE.   No time at all?

As they go the BUCKET AND CLOTH MAN
and the GREEN LADY *go by. He is weak and
stumbling. The* BLACK DOG *follows them off.
The* DEPRESSED GIRL *goes on sitting.*

A BUSINESSMAN *with a* THRUMPIN *riding on
his back. He doesn't know it's there. The* GIRL

leaves. He is joined by colleagues, all with
THRUMPINS, *for a meeting. They are talking
but we can't hear what they say. All we can hear
is a shrill twittering wordless conversation
among the* THRUMPINS. *Still* PASSERBY
dancing.

A smart WOMAN *in mid thirties. It is the*
SKRIKER.

SKRIKER.   So the Skriker sought fame and fortune telling,
celebrity knockout drops, TV stardomination, chat
showdown and market farces, see if I carefree,
and completely forgetmenot Lily and Josie.
Lovely and Kissie, silly and cosy, lived in peaces
and quite, Crossie still mad as a hitter and Lively
soon gave happy birth to a baby a booby a babbly
byebye booboo boohoo hooooo. What a blossom
bless'em. Dear little mighty.

LILY *and* JOSIE *and the baby are on the sofa.*
RAWHEADANDBLOODYBONES *sits on a
shelf watching, invisible to them.* SKRIKER *and*
MEN *with* THRUMPINS *leave.*

LILY.   Everyone says you'll be tired or they . . . bunnies
or fluffy . . . everything too sweet and you think
that's really boring, makes you want to dress her
in black but she's not sweet like pink and blue. Or
you get them moaning about never get enough
sleep or oh my stitches or like that, no one lets on.

JOSIE.   Are you listening to me?

LILY.   Day and night.

JOSIE.   But in fact never.

LILY.   I'm tired.

JOSIE.   You just said tired wasn't it.

LILY.   It's not all about it but I'm still tired.

JOSIE.   So what's the big secret?

LILY.   Not a secret.

JOSIE.	What's so wonderful wonderful only you're brilliant enough to feel it?
LILY.	Nothing.
JOSIE.	Everyone gets born you know. It's not something you invented. Walk down the street you'll see several people that were born.
	Silence.
LILY.	So tell me again.
	Silence.
	Josie, it's over.
JOSIE.	How can it be over if it didn't happen?
LILY.	What you thought what you dreamed whatever is over.
JOSIE.	But I did go.
LILY.	Josie, I was with you all the time.
JOSIE.	But I did go.
LILY.	All right.
JOSIE.	Smash your face in. I did go. They need us you know, they think we're magic. They drink your blood. I miss the dancing.
	Silence.
JOSIE.	So what is it about her?
LILY.	I know everyone's born. I can't help it. Everything's shifted round so she's in the middle. I never minded things. But everything dangerous seems it might get her. I know she's just . . . But if she wasn't all right it'd be a waste, wouldn't it.
JOSIE.	What happened to me is like that. As big as that is to you. I promise.
LILY.	But it happened in no time at all.
JOSIE.	Yes. But where I was it was years.
LILY.	Yes.

JOSIE.   All right then.

LILY.   And it's over now.

JOSIE.   Everything's flat here like a video. There's something watching us.

LILY.   Yes but there's not.

JOSIE.   I can't go back because they hate me for getting away.

LILY.   You want to go back?

JOSIE.   I'm never going to be all right.

LILY.   You know how they say 'oh their little fingers' and of course they've got little fingers, they couldn't have fingers like us. But that's not what they mean. I mean look at her fingers.

JOSIE.   She's a changeling.

LILY.   She what?

JOSIE.   That's not your baby. They've put one of theirs and taken yours off.

LILY.   Don't say that, don't.

JOSIE.   Changeling. / Changeling.

LILY.   I warn you, I'll kill you / don't say it,

JOSIE.   You believe me don't you?

LILY.   I don't want, I don't believe you no / but I

JOSIE.   Lucky for them.

LILY.   don't want to hear it.

JOSIE.   They'll keep yours down there. It makes them stronger. They'll breed from it. And you'll always have this one watching you. Look at its little slitty eye.

LILY.   Don't even think it. / I'm not listening.

JOSIE.   Shall I tell you what? if you want your own one back? You put the changeling on a shovel and put it in the fire, that's what they used to do. So we'd

use the cooker and put it over the gas. And
sometimes they turn into a cat and go up the
chimney. How'd it get out of here? Round and
round the walls. I'll open the window. Then you
get your own one back in the cot.

LILY.   I can't live with you if you're like this.

JOSIE.   You've got to fight them. You say you love her
and you won't even do something to get her back.
This isn't human. I can tell.

LILY.   Whatever you are, if you're really there, if you
can hear me, I want a wish.

JOSIE.   She'll come back, look out.

LILY.   I wish Josie wasn't mad.

JOSIE.   Don't wish me.

           Silence.

LILY.   Did anything happen?

JOSIE.   What have you done?

LILY.   What have I done?

JOSIE.   Hurts.

LILY.   Where? what?

JOSIE.   Inside.

LILY.   What have they done to you?

JOSIE.   Here.

LILY.   I wish –

JOSIE.   Don't don't don't.

LILY.   What have they done?

JOSIE.   I don't think anything's broken. They haven't
really put bits of metal. I killed her. Did I? Yes.
I hadn't forgotten but. She was just as precious.
Yours isn't the only. If I hadn't she'd still. I keep
knowing it again, what can I do? Why did I?
It should have been me. Because under that pain

oh shit there's under that under that there's this other / under that there's –

LILY.   Wait, stop, I'm sorry, I'll / fix it

JOSIE.   Don't let me feel it. It's coming for me. Hide me. This is what. When I killed her. What I was frightened. Trying to stop when I. It's here.

LILY.   No please I'll –

JOSIE.   Save me. Can you? There's no one to save.

LILY.   I wish –

JOSIE.   No.

LILY.   If I wish you happy, no, you could kill people and still, don't feel pain no, just all right what does that mean, I wish I hadn't, no I'd do it again, I wish you were like before I wished, does that, I wish –

JOSIE.   You mustn't keep wishing or she'll get you.

LILY.   Are you all right now?

JOSIE.   There's something.

LILY.   What?

JOSIE.   Gone.

LILY.   It doesn't hurt?

JOSIE.   What? (*Silence.*)

LILY.   I should have asked you.

JOSIE.   Well ask me.

LILY.   If you really thought . . .

JOSIE.   Are you starting again? I was there for years.

LILY.   No, if you thought she was a changeling.

JOSIE.   Shall we do some tests? Yeah? Be a laugh.

LILY.   No we won't. We'll take care of her.

JOSIE.   Have you been wishing? Stupid. She'll get you now.

Many couples dancing. They include KELPIE *and* WOMAN, GREEN LADY *and* BUCKET MAN, *who is weak,* BROWNIE, SKRIKER *as man,* RAWHEADANDBLOODYBONES, BLACK DOG, JOHNNY SQUAREFOOT, NELLIE LONGARMS. *There is a large shoe and when they've finished dancing they climb on it. It is identical to* LILY's *shoe which she has kicked off. She is sitting on the sofa with a* MAN *about 30. It is the* SKRIKER. JOSIE *is chopping vegetables. The* BABY *is in a carrycot.*

SKRIKER.   I'd wait down the end of the road and see you come out with the pram. I'd watch you in the park.

LILY.   When did you?

SKRIKER.   You knew I was there though.

LILY.   No, when?

SKRIKER.   You meant me to follow you or I wouldn't have done it.

LILY.   I never saw you.

SKRIKER.   Unconsciously meant. Or in your stars. Some deep . . .

LILY.   Oh like that.

SKRIKER.   Yes some fateful . . . So that when we met it wasn't for the first time. You felt that. Some people are meant to be together. I'd walk out of meetings because of this overpowering . . . I'd accelerate to fifty on a short block up to a red light. Anything that wasn't you my eyes veered off. I couldn't sleep, of course, not that sleep's my best – do you sleep?

LILY.   If she lets me.

SKRIKER.   How do you do that? No what do you do, tell me. You go to bed.

LILY.   I go to bed.

SKRIKER.   You take anything?

LILY.   Not to sleep, no, be a waste.

SKRIKER.   So you just lie down.

LILY.   I might look at a magazine for about ten minutes but then I'm too sleepy.

SKRIKER.   So what's that like when you get sleepy?

LILY.   You know what it's like.

SKRIKER.   No, what's it like.

JOSIE *goes out.*

LILY.   My eyes keep shutting by themselves. I'm reading something and then I see my eyes are shut so I open them and think I'll just finish that story and the words are going double so I don't bother. So I put out the light.

SKRIKER.   And then what?

LILY.   I go to sleep.

SKRIKER.   No, how? What happens.

LILY.   I'm lying there. And . . .

SKRIKER.   And thoughts.

LILY.   Maybe thoughts a bit about the day or –

SKRIKER.   Rush through your head.

LILY.   Not rush but . . . and I might see things.

SKRIKER.   See . . . ?

LILY.   Like a tree with its leaves or somebody . . .

SKRIKER.   Frightening things?

LILY.   No but nothing to do with anything, not dreams exactly but bright – and I know something I've just thought isn't right, like maybe there's two things that seem to be something to do with each other but they're not but I can't remember what it was –

SKRIKER.   Your mind's going out of control like when there's going to be an accident. / When any

LILY.   No.

SKRIKER.   minute people are going to be mangled in some machinery and it's going very slowly but you can't / stop it.

LILY.   No, not like that.

SKRIKER.   Like what?

LILY.   Nothing, I'm asleep after that.

SKRIKER.   So maybe that's something I'd pick up. I'd slide off into sleep beside you.

LILY.   Why don't you sleep?

SKRIKER.   I have slept. It's partly my legs, they can't get right. And things in my head. Well I'll tell you there was this . . . He was quite highpowered, he thought he was. He was going to help me, he was going to manage me because I was a conjuror at this point, I could do these amazing – I was entitled to recognition. He didn't deliver. So I'd lie awake. Well he subsequently died in fact. So that was good. But I've got a lot on my mind. You'll help me with that.

LILY.   I don't know.

SKRIKER.   Yes because you have faith in me.

JOSIE *comes back.*

Have you noticed the large number of meteorological phenomena lately? Earthquakes. Volcanoes. Drought. Apocalyptic meteorological phenomena. The increase of sickness. It was always possible to think whatever your personal problem, there's always nature. Spring will return even if it's without me. Nobody loves me but at least it's a sunny day. This has been a comfort to people as long as they've existed. But it's not available any more. Sorry. Nobody loves me and

the sun's going to kill me. Spring will return and
nothing will grow. Some people might feel
concerned about that. But it makes me feel
important. I'm going to be around when the world
as we know it ends. I'm going to witness
unprecedented catastrophe. I like a pileup on the
motorway. I like the kind of war we're having
lately. I like snuff movies. But this is going to be
the big one.

JOSIE *goes out.*

Your friend doesn't like me.

LILY.   I'm sorry.

SKRIKER.   I'm getting uncomfortable.

LILY.   She doesn't like anyone.

SKRIKER.   I can't tolerate being disliked. So never mind.
We'll go away together. You'd like a holiday.
We'll bring the baby, no problem, I love kids,
babies are cupid. What are you doing tomorrow?

LILY.   No, I –

SKRIKER.   You think this is sudden. I think it's sudden. No I
don't. I've been looking for you. It's going to
happen.

LILY.   What's going to happen?

SKRIKER.   Us being together forever. We both know that. So
there's no point taking a long time getting to the
point which we got to the first time no even
before we met no even before I ever set eyes on
you because this kind of thing is meant. Don't
you agree?

LILY.   Yes I do. I think I do.

SKRIKER.   What's this 'I think'?

LILY.   I just . . .

SKRIKER.   Are you backing out?

LILY.   No. What? I –

SKRIKER.   Don't do this to me. I warn you. Quite
            straightforwardly as one human being to another.

LILY.   I didn't mean –

SKRIKER.   Don't don't don't don't don't look startled.
            You're the only good person I've ever met.
            Everyone else has tried to destroy me. But you
            wish me well. You wouldn't deny that.

LILY.   No, I –

SKRIKER.   No.

LILY.   No I –

SKRIKER.   What? what? don't dare. This is a high voltage
            cable. Are you going to grab it? I'm going to take
            care of you and the baby. You're coming with me.
            You don't have to worry about anything any
            more.

            JOSIE *comes in again.*

LILY.   I do like you. I can't look away from you. But a
            bit slower. It's no use getting angry because I
            can't –

SKRIKER.   I hate it when I'm so unkind. This sometimes
            happens. I won't go into my childhood just now. I
            can't forgive myself. I feel terrible.

LILY.   I didn't mean –

SKRIKER.   I'm useless, I get something beautiful and I ruin
            it. Everything I touch falls apart. There are some
            people who deserve to be killed and I believe
            it's important to be completely without remorse.
            I admire that if someone has no compassion
            because that's what it takes. But other people
            such as yourself. You won't want to see me again.
            How could I do that? I worship you. I'm so
            ashamed. I feel sick. Help me. Forgive me. Could
            you ever love me?

            JOSIE *attacks him with a knife, slashing his arm
            and chest. Blood on his shirt.*

Do you love me? Do you love me?

LILY.   Yes, yes I do.

He takes off the bloodstained shirt and tie. Underneath, identical clean ones.

SKRIKER   (*to* JOSIE). You're getting into a lot of trouble. She loves me.

LILY.   No I don't. What are you?

SKRIKER.   But you do you know. See you later.

He goes.

LILY.   These things only come because of you. Go and live somewhere else.

GREEN LADY *pushing* BUCKET MAN *in a wheelchair.*

KELPIE *with the body of* WOMAN *who went away with him.*

TELESCOPE GIRL *distraught and searching.* JOSIE *leaves with* BLACK DOG.

PASSERBY *still dancing.*

MARIE, *a young woman about* LILY's *age, is visiting* LILY. *It is the* SKRIKER. *The* KELPIE *cuts up the woman's body.*

SKRIKER.   Can I pick up the baby?

LILY.   No.

SKRIKER.   Sorry.

LILY.   I don't remember you.

SKRIKER.   I've grown up.

Silence.

Someone's going to kill me. Marie never hung out with the right people. I need somewhere to stay.

LILY.   I can't help you.

SKRIKER.   You're not the only person I know. I'm almost a

celebrity. My face has been on the covers – not
this face exactly but a face. But I'm the same old
Marie. Those are silver, these are gold. There's a
lot of people out there who pretend to be your
friend. They say they are. But you and me and
Josie swore in blood.

LILY.   I don't remember.

SKRIKER.   You remember the waste ground? you remember
the corner with the nettles? you remember Josie?

LILY.   Of course I remember Josie.

SKRIKER.   You've forgotten Marie.

LILY.   I'm sorry . . . I can't . . . I'm not sure.

SKRIKER.   When we left messages in the wall?

LILY.   Yes I do remember the wall.

SKRIKER.   The tree.

LILY.   Corner shop after school.

SKRIKER.   Sherbet lemons.

LILY.   But were you . . . ?

SKRIKER.   It's funny how much of our life we forget. You
can't help it. You never liked me best. Let me
stay with you. There's room now Josie's gone. I'd
be safe here.

LILY.   No.

SKRIKER.   My dad did things to me. I never told you that.
My mum shut me in the cupboard.

LILY.   Go somewhere else.

SKRIKER.   My boyfriend's going to kill me.

LILY.   You're not Marie.

SKRIKER.   No, but I'm still in danger. That's why I came.
Look, I'm not pretending anything. That's good
isn't it? You've got to love me.

LILY.   How would that help?

SKRIKER.   Yes, help me Lily. I don't work properly.
            You've got to come with me. You can save me.
            You want to.

LILY.   I don't love you at all. I don't like you. I don't
            care if you die. I'm never going to see you again.

            SKRIKER *goes.* LILY *sits exhausted. Later she
            goes.*

            A FAMILY *having a picnic on a beach.
            The beach is covered with* BLUE MEN.
            PASSERBY *still dancing.*

            JOSIE *and the* BLACK DOG *are in a small
            room, visited by a shabby respectable* MAN
            about 40. It is the SKRIKER.

JOSIE.   She didn't know anyone. She didn't have
            anywhere to stay the night. I slipped a wire loop
            over her head.

            SKRIKER *laughs.*

            So that'll do for a bit, yeh? You'll feel ok. There's
            an earthquake on the telly last night. There's a
            motorway pileup in the fog.

SKRIKER.   You're a good girl, Josie.

JOSIE.   There's dead children.

SKRIKER.   Tell me more about her.

JOSIE.   She had red hair. She had big feet. She liked
            biscuits. She woke up while I was doing it. But
            you didn't do the carcrash. You'd tell me. You're
            not strong enough to do an earthquake.

            SKRIKER *coughs.*

            I'll do terrible things, I promise. Just leave it to
            me. You don't have to do anything. Don't do
            anything. Promise.

            SKRIKER *coughs.*

            You won't do anything to Lily?

SKRIKER.   Who's Lily?

JOSIE.   Nobody. Someone you used to know. You've forgotten her.

SKRIKER laughs.

Have you forgotten her?

SKRIKER coughs.

I think you'd like me to do something tomorrow.

SKRIKER coughs.

The BUCKET MAN *comes slowly in his wheelchair, moving it himself now. He stops and dozes. The* TELESCOPE GIRL *comes in, she has bandaged wrists.* RAWHEADANDBLOODY-BONES, KELPIE *and* JOHNNY SQUAREFOOT *rush across wildly, tangling with the* PASSERBY, *who keeps dancing.*

SKRIKER.   Josie went further and murther in the dark, trying to keep the Skriker sated seated besotted with gobbets, tossing it giblets, to stop it from wolfing, stop it engulfing. But still there was gobbling and gabbling, giggling and gaggling, biting and beating, eating and hating, hooting and looting and lightning and thunder in the southeast northwest northeast southwest northsouth crisis. Lily doolalley was living in peacetime, no more friend, no more fiend, safe as dollshouses. But she worried and sorried and lay awake into the nightmare. Poor furry, she thought, pure feary, where are you now and then? And something drove her over and over and out of her mind how you go.

BLACK ANNIS *has small houses in a glass aquarium. She slowly fills it with water.*

LILY, *with the* BABY, *arrives at the hospital, where there is a very ill old woman. It is the* SKRIKER.

LILY.   What you doing in hospital? If you're really
         asleep I'll say it again after. I thought you'd be in
         the government or the movies by now. I went to
         stations when people were coming off trains or
         closing time coming out of pubs. I'd put her in the
         pram, she'd go back to sleep. There are things out
         in the night. I think you should be glad I've come,
         and open your eyes. When I made you go I didn't
         know you'd really gone, anyone spoke to me I
         was frightened. Then one day there was someone
         going to jump from a building and when it wasn't
         you I started looking.

SKRIKER.   Don't kill me.

LILY.   It's Lily.

SKRIKER.   They've taken my friends away. Not me.

LILY.   I'll take care of you.

SKRIKER.   You're a liar, Lily.

LILY.   I came to find you.

SKRIKER.   I had a friend fed her cat on tins and it was
            frightened of real food. Put a bit of raw meat
            down and it leapt back. It smelt blood. Thought it
            was going to eat it. The dinner the cat. I've
            enemies in here. Shh.

LILY.   I came to say I'd go with you.

SKRIKER.   Where are you going, dear?

LILY.   You said you wanted me to. Like Josie.

SKRIKER.   I've no idea who these people are.

LILY.   Yes because I miss . . . You'll leave everyone else
         alone if I do that, I'm not bringing the baby so
         don't ask, you're to leave her alone always. And
         Josie alone. Because if I go it'll help, won't it?

SKRIKER.   Have you tried dialling 999?

LILY.   I know I said I didn't love you.

SKRIKER.   Aren't you afraid a fade away?

LILY.   No because if it's what Josie did I'll be back in no
            time. It could feel like hundreds of years and I
            wouldn't leave the baby for five minutes but
            when I get back she won't know I've gone.

SKRIKER.   Gone with the wind hover crafty.

LILY.   Even if it's a nightmare. I'll be back the same
            second. I'll make you safe. Take me with you.

            *SKRIKER leaps up. It is no longer the old
            woman. It is the SKRIKER from the beginning of
            the piece, but full of energy.*

SKRIKER.   Lily, my heartthrobber baron, my solo flighty,
            now I've some blood in my all in veins, now I've
            some light in my lifeline nightline nightlight a
            candle to light you to bedlam, here comes a –

            SKRIKER lights a candle and gives it to LILY

            Watch the lightyear. Here you stand in an
            enchanted wood you or wouldn't you. Just hold
            this candle the scandal I said and she stood till
            stood still stood till what?

            *LILY stands holding the candle. Everything else
            is dark. A blackbird sings.*

            *An OLD WOMAN and a DEFORMED GIRL
            sitting together. They see LILY appear. The
            GIRL cries out. The candle goes out and LILY
            sees them.*

            *The SKRIKER is the ancient creature it was at
            the beginning of the piece. The PASSERBY is
            still dancing.*

            Lily appeared like a ghastly, made their hair stand
            on endless night, their blood run fast. 'Am I in
            fairylanded?' she wandered. 'No, said the old
            crony, 'this is the real world' whirl whir wh wh
            what is this? Lily was solid flash. If she was back
            on earth where on earth where was the rockabye
            baby gone the treetop? Lost and gone for
            everybody was dead years and tears ago, it was

another cemetery, a black whole hundred yearns.
Grief struck by lightning. And this old dear me
was Lily's granddaughter what a horror storybook
ending. 'Oh I was tricked tracked wracked,' cried
our heroine distress, 'I hoped to save the worldly,
I hoped I'd make the fury better than she should
be.' And what would be comfy of her now? She
didn't know if she ate a mortal morsel she'd
crumble to dust panic. Are you my grand great
grand great are you my child's child's child's?
But when the daughters grand and great greater
greatest knew she was from the distant past
master class, then rage raging bullfight bullroar.

The GIRL *bellows wordless rage at* LILY.

'Oh they couldn't helpless,' said the
granddaughter, 'they were stupid stupefied
stewpotbellied not evil weevil devil take the
hindmost of them anyway.' But the child hated
the monstrous.

GIRL *bellows.*

'Leave her alone poor little soul-o', said the grin
dafter, 'cold in the headache, shaking and
shocking. Have a what drink, wrap her in a
blanket out, have a sandwhich one would you
like?' So Lily bit off more than she could choose.
And she was dustbin.

The OLD WOMAN *holds out some food and*
LILY *puts out her hand to take it.*

The PASSERBY *stops dancing.*

End.